DISCARD

Childsong, Monksong

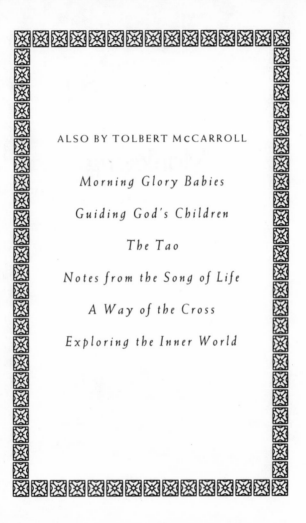

ALSO BY TOLBERT McCARROLL

Morning Glory Babies

Guiding God's Children

The Tao

Notes from the Song of Life

A Way of the Cross

Exploring the Inner World

Childsong, Monksong

A Spiritual Journey

TOLBERT McCARROLL

ST. MARTIN'S PRESS
NEW YORK

ISBN 0-312-11253-X

First Edition: September 1994
10 9 8 7 6 5 4 3 2 1

*Grateful acknowledgment is made to the following for permission
to reprint previously published materials.*

The lines from Rilke in Chapter 4 are from the poem "Erinnerung"
("Memory"). Rainer Maria Rilke, *Selected Poems. Bilingual Edition*, trans./
ed. by MacIntyre, C. F. Copyright © 1940, 1968 C. F. MacIntyre.
(Berkeley: University of California Press, 1968), page 40.

T. S. Eliot's lines from *Little Gidding* in Chapter 13 are excerpts from
"Little Gidding" in FOUR QUARTETS, copyright © 1943 by T. S.
Eliot and renewed 1971 by Esme Valerie Eliot, reprinted by permission
of Harcourt Brace & Company.

The quote from Bede Griffiths in Chapter 15 is taken from his book
The Marriage of East and West (Springfield, IL: Templegate Publishers,
1982), pp. 42–43.

The closing haiku following Chapter 19 appears as it was translated
by Nobuyuki Yuasa in *The Year of My Life, A Translation of Issa's 'Oraga
Haru,'* 2nd edition. Copyright © 1972 The Regents of the University
of California. (Berkeley: University of California Press, 1972), p. 140.

The author is also grateful for insight provided into several other
poems and prose sections by that work and by Cliff Edwards' *Issa, The
Story of a Poet-Priest* (Tokyo: Macmillan Shuppan KK, 1985).

Dedicated to

Sato
1818–1819
JAPAN

Tina
1988–1991
UNITED STATES

Dana Rica
1988–
ROMANIA–UNITED STATES

"Those the gods love, go home early."
—from a memorial to Mozart

Dear Reader,

You and I travel through secret countries. In our journeys we both have come upon a few idyllic sites and many frightening abysses. For every person there are different hells. Mine have recently included the death of children I love, the AIDS epidemic in the United States and Romania, the hostility of individuals, rejection by church leadership, the crumbling of my personal defenses, the glare of public attention, conflicts between personal grief and public obligations. This cluster of infernos was unique to me. But one thing I share with you, and every woman and man in history, is the often torturous struggle to keep moving toward a place of inner harmony.

I hunger for a contemplative life. I am also a father to children. This is my anchor in reality. People know me as "brother Toby." Once, when I was taking an evening walk with three-year-old Holly, a stranger approached me. "Brother Toby?" he inquired. "No," said Holly before I could respond. "He is brother Daddy!" With that she took my hand and led me away from the puzzled man.

Holly was right. I am a monk and a father. In that combination there are and will be many hardships, and there is also to be found the joyful path to my happiness and spiritual fulfillment. In the pages that follow are the stories of two children who never met yet were made sisters by a deadly plague. One, my daughter Tina, helped me hear a profound call to find a simple way to the mystery we know as "God." The other, my goddaughter Dana Rica, helped me become for a brief moment the hands of God in a place where children were forgotten. Then Tina died and my way was dark.

My journey values the spiritual. But spirituality and madness are parallel forces that are much more related to each other than is often acknowledged. A sojourn on either subjective path is a passport to the other. For many months I crossed back and forth.

It became necessary to surrender to the madness of death before I could be made whole. In that process Tina and Dana Rica are crucial. So is an ancient city of peace, people I have learned to love, a Japanese haiku poet, and perhaps also a big blue whale named Philip.

After writing the first draft of this story, I discovered that I did not want to share it all with you. My emotions were raw and unhealed. The desire for privacy was natural. But the only justification for writing a memoir is that it becomes a means for others to explore their own experiences at some deep level. The decision to go on writing was also a decision for me to see my own experience in terms of our common adventure.

There are many quiet moments in what follows. As the story unfolds there are also a number of startling situations. But, like you, I suspect, I live in the ordinary times and only survive the dramatic events. And, in the final analysis, all we really have to share with each other is how we live.

TOLBERT McCARROLL

Childsong,
Monksong

I live in northern California's Sonoma County. It is an earthly paradise known, long before the Europeans came, as one of God's happy dwelling places. Clean streams twist playfully through forested hills until they merge with the nearby mighty ocean. As yet we have not spoiled it too much.

This is a place where dreamers come. My home is on a little farm. Two decades ago I came here from San Francisco with two others to find God in the daily rhythm of a simple life. That was our dream. We are lay monastics in the Catholic tradition. A few miles away is a monastery of Americans searching for fulfillment in the tradition of Tibetan Buddhism. That is their dream. Others have come in search of adventure and material gain: the Russians in 1812, the Spanish soon afterward. Today stockbrokers become farmers in hopes of making fortunes by raising the right grapes for expensive wines. There are many things we all have in common. Most of us are refugees. The thrifty and industrious Italians came from

Tuscany in the 1800s. In this century energetic and creative gays poured out of the cities and formed an enclave along the Russian River where they hoped to live in peace.

All my neighbors define part of their treasure in terms of the songs of birds and the smiles of children. Sonoma County's most famous citizen today is the cartoonist Charles M. Schulz. Year after year his Peanuts characters proclaim that "happiness is a warm puppy." I agree with that gospel. My cozy nest in paradise is what I want. I have no desire to be concerned about anything else. Peace is what I prize. Trouble is not something I seek. But to live is also to know pain and fear.

My pain is usually related to loss, and that is an unavoidable part of life. Like everyone else, I construct the comfortable myth that my private world is happy, eternal, and carefree. When death occurs, especially the death of a child, the myth is shattered. I lost a little daughter to AIDS. Her name was Tina. My world was bleak and arid after her death. It took time for hope to be renewed. Even when my life had been revitalized, the fearful ghost of my past loss continually robbed me of inner comfort. I saw this troublesome emotional attitude as a weakness.

I was surprised. In the art of living I had been successful. It never occurred to me there would be emotional and spiritual afflictions I could not handle. It is, however, inevitable that everyone encounters overpowering circumstances. Mine was a deeply painful odyssey in which children suffered. However, there is nothing fundamentally unique in my journey. All people will experience situations where the human spirit is in danger of destruction. Many, like myself, will be unaware of the peril until they have been hurt. But no matter what hazard we encounter or how vulnerable we may be, for most of us the road goes on. And we rediscover ways that lead to deep satisfaction with life.

In recent years the story of my life has re-volved around a spiritual family called Star-cross Community. It began when I joined with Marti Aggeler and Julie DeRossi, the com-munity's first sisters. We all came from Cath-olic backgrounds, with significant stopovers in Asian spirituality and humanistic psychology.

In 1976 we established a small Christmas tree farm in rural Sonoma County. We take tradi-tional vows of poverty, celibacy, and perma-nent commitment to a contemplative lifestyle. Our reception from the official Catholic hier-archy is frequently warm, sometimes a nervous toleration, and occasionally hostile. However, our acceptance in the broader Catholic fel-lowship, especially among contemplative com-munities, is consistently empathetic and fra-ternal. Our guidebooks are the Gospels and St. Benedict's monastic rule.

The greatest challenge of my life came from the children adopted by the Starcross Com-munity after I had turned fifty-five. All but one of our children had tested positive to the presence of HIV, the virus which causes AIDS, when they came to us.

At first it may seem that being a monk and a father or mother do not go together. Certainly the Roman Catholic hierarchy generally believes that parenting is inconsistent with a monastic vocation.

But children have been happily raised by celibate parents, and their presence has transformed many a religious institution into a family. The outstanding example of this in the United States has been the experience of the Protestant monastic communities commonly known as the Shakers, where thousands of children were nourished. But even the fifth-century Rule of St. Benedict refers to children. One chapter is devoted exclusively to requiring that the elderly and children "be treated with kindly consideration." In other sections practical matters are addressed, such as keeping *"pueri parvi"*—small boys—under supervision at the dinner table. No parent would dispute the wisdom there.

Is it fair to the child to grow up with a father or mother who goes to the chapel and sings psalms several times a day? Yes. There are no inherent evils in a spiritual environment. It all depends on the people. Are there conflicts? Yes. And in such cases a parent's obligation to a child must come first. But serious tension is rare. I have come to believe that for me the contemplative dimension in my life is making me a better parent, and certainly children have given my spiritual life a needed balance.

My experience with parenting began in the early 1960s. I had married Claire Cordier during my last year of law school. A few years later Claire and I adopted two children. Tamar and Duncan had been born in war areas, Korea and Greece. Claire was a diabetic with heart problems and died in her middle years. Later, after my son and daughter were grown and I was a part of the Starcross Community, I became a joint foster parent to Kevin, Marlene, Ethan, and Eileen. The four children were from very difficult backgrounds. Two of them had serious medical problems. They all came to us young. When the last one graduated from high school, twelve years later, I thought my parenting was over. But it was just beginning.

The story of how we responded to the AIDS crisis among children was recounted by the media, in Bob Elfstrom's film *Christmas at Starcross* and in my book *Morning Glory Babies: Children with AIDS and the Celebration of Life.* Many people have come to know of Nicki, whom Marti took out of a hospital crib where she had been confined needlessly for over two years; David, the budding violinist, who is not infected: Michelle, our bouncy seven-year-old; Tina; Holly, who was HIV positive but is now showing no evidence of AIDS; Josh, who died from AIDS a few days following his first birthday; and Andrew, who was born after Tina's death, and who also tested positive to HIV at birth.

I have never doubted that my personal vocation is to a contemplative lifestyle, but I have often put my calling to the test. The AIDS epidemic threw me into unfamiliar spiritual turbulence, which reached gale force when I responded to the cruel plight of children with AIDS in Romania. The story of my efforts to establish home care for thirty Romanian children appeared on national television. It was presented as a success story. The millions of viewers never saw the dark side. By the time I discovered there was a price to be paid for what I had seen and done, the TV crews had, thankfully, moved on to other interests. But from the beginning they knew, as well as I, that at the center of the story was a delicate little girl.

Tina's birth mother, now dead from AIDS, came from a Catholic family that included a nun and a priest. Already sick, she asked us to adopt her child. Julie was present at Tina's birth and brought her home a few days later. I had no warning that this was to be a turning point in my life. But I now realize that every child we love requires us to follow a new path.

3

Sharing Tina's life was a unique and profound experience. I was fifty-seven when she was born and sixty when she died. During those months I started to question the direction in which I was traveling and learned to listen again to an inner song I had almost forgotten.

Tina ruled our family like a little princess. Hers was a domain deeply committed to love. After Tina's death Julie wrote this description of her daughter:

Tina was happy and sure of herself, cute and charming, a bright, whimsical pixie, who made every day delightful. She loved music and dancing. She was always ready for celebrations, which she called "happies." Nature fascinated Tina, especially birds and stars. She liked times of family prayer and being in the chapel.

Tina was and is the daughter I always wanted. From the day of her birth I knew it. She was not some unfortunate baby I took care of. I received from her more than I gave. Tina played many roles in our family. For several years she was the cherished baby. Then when a new little one arrived she became the concerned older sister. She took upon herself the task of interpreting the baby's wishes to the adults.

She had her daddy wrapped around her little finger. Whatever important issues he was handling would be dropped in a minute if Tina suggested going to feed the ducks or playing marbles.

Tina was an authentic person who demanded respect from those around her. She would not be treated as a generic toddler, or even worse a generic patient. If anyone did not treat her properly it was "Away, away!" and with an imperial flick of the wrist she'd banish them from her presence.

And what a brave little trooper, especially in regard to walking. Physically, nothing came easy for Tina. However, the fact that her legs and feet didn't work without clumsy braces never slowed her down. She was determined and stubborn. She wanted to walk, and gave it all she had with great good humor. In fact, with absolute joy.

Sometimes I'd catch a glimpse of a stranger watching her. They'd smile sympathetically as this cheerful little cherub trudged by. And I'd think to myself, if only you understood. This is not some poor crippled child to be pitied. This is a world-class athlete in training. She could win an Olympic gold medal for what she's doing here. And I'd feel so tremendously proud of her.

The HIV virus was continually weakening Tina's defenses. The count of important cells in her blood started a serious decline before she was eighteen months old. After her second Christmas the doctor warned that the numbers were dropping fast. Tina was born in Hawaii, and the islands were Julie's idea of the promised land. Outwardly both she and Tina were in great shape. It seemed a perfect time for a trip to Maui. They had a splendid holiday and came back full of memories of warm beaches and whales. Julie has a deep reverence for these giant and gentle creatures. On this trip humpback whales were everywhere Julie and Tina went. They had come to give birth to their young. Mothers and children, whales and human, frolicked in the warm waters.

Just before Easter Tina's cell count dropped very low. Even though it was not a surprise, it was nonetheless devastating to hear the figures. Besides, Tina had a fungal infection that would not go away. She was listless. Julie took her to the university doctors in San Francisco and talked to people around the country. There were no new therapies on the horizon and nothing new to suggest. Julie was drowning in the realization that she could not protect Tina from getting sick.

The weather at the farm was superb for Holy Week and Easter. Apple blossoms were in full bloom. It was simple to feel the presence of God. Tina and Julie were never far from our minds as we celebrated the beginning moments of our faith—when death did not have the final word.

During Holy Week Julie had an experience. Perhaps she dozed and it was a dream. Perhaps it was something else. This is how she remembered it.

I'm on the beach at MauiLu. It's late afternoon. I can feel the sun and the wind. I'm wearing white.

I look to my left for a path down the beach. I can't see it. I look out to sea and near the horizon see a giant blue whale. I know he's called Philip. I am drawn to him. I'm awestruck at his size and power. He's the color of the sea. We go under where it's dark. We're immersed in ocean sound.

I know where he lives. It is very deep. He is wise. I want to get with this old whale and go very deep.

I remember painful images of the last few days. When I heard Tina's cell count I felt so helpless. I thought the ocean is coming to claim her and what can I do about it?

Then, later, with the waves of grief I thought of a pole stuck near shore. Tina and I were clinging to it while the sea raged around us. The waves crashed in and out. Our clothes were in tatters. We were defeated. I didn't think we could hold on much longer.

Somehow our whale friend is a great comfort. His reality is in a different dimension. If my baby can be with him deep in the ocean, underneath the stars, it will be all right. I can be there too. We can all be there together.

God has appeared in many forms throughout our history. On at least one occasion He or She was a blue whale named Philip.

4

One of my perennial sources of inspiration has been the spiritual sojourn of Issa, a haiku poet who died in 1827. Throughout his troubled life Issa was searching for beauty. One of his most poignant poems contains only a few words in the original Japanese: "loveliness," "rip/shoji screen," "milky way." I read it this way:

> *How lovely it is*
> *to look through the broken window*
> *and discover the Milky Way.*

It is not easy to look beyond the broken window of a shattering loss and experience the wholeness of the Milky Way. Issa hungered for beauty, peace, and harmony. But he had to find those graces while surrounded by sickness and decay.

Sato was Issa's daughter. She was born in 1818, when Issa was fifty-seven. "Sato" means "wisdom." She was well named. On his daughter's first birthday Issa wrote, "I am ashamed to admit that my little child of one year is closer to the truth than I." He contrasted his "meaningless activity" with the endless moments of peace, grace, and joy in Sato's life.

Sato's father had been a lonely man whose poetry captured the spiritual isolation of the human condition. At fifty he fulfilled a lifetime desire and returned to the small farmhouse of his childhood. Issa married Kiku, a young village woman. Their first child died soon after birth. Another baby, Sato, was born in May. Her first year brought great joy. The child was the center of Issa's universe. He rejoiced in every little ordinary but miraculous event of her active life. "She is pure moonlight, beaming from head to toe. . . ." To live in the presence of such vitality is to experience again the freshness of life. "Watching her, I forget my age and my corrupt past."

It was the custom for Japanese poets to travel. Shortly after his daughter's first birthday, Issa took to the road. But soon a foreboding brought him back home. Sato was seriously ill. A variola virus had attacked and her immune system was collapsing. The frightening signs of smallpox were covering her beautiful young body. Only a few days before Issa had mused that in time she would learn to dance and "her dancing will be lovelier than celestial music!" Now high fevers struck down the little dancer. Issa's pain was acute. He cried out

> Why is my child dying? She has just begun to taste life. She ought to be as fresh and green as the new needles on the everlasting pine. Why must she lie here on her deathbed, with festering lesions, caught in the vile grip of the god of pox? I am her father and can hardly bear to watch her fade away—a little more each day—like a pure blossom in a rainstorm.

The virus robbing Sato of her life was known as early as 1122 B.C. and not eradicated until 1977. Over three thousand years of smallpox plagues claimed untold millions of victims. Each statistic was the destruction of a unique universe of human experience and expectations.

Sato rallied for a while. Issa and Kiku rejoiced. But soon hope faded. "She grew weaker until on June 21st, as the morning glories closed their petals, she closed her eyes forever. Her mother held the cold body and cried out in unremitting pain."

Emotional attachment was not encouraged in Issa's spiritual tradition. He had been taught to avoid investing his energy in worldly matters, which disappear like dew on the grass. However, these religious doctrines could not withstand the experience of death. "I tried hard, but I could not break the bonds of human love." He wrote:

> This world of dew
> Is nothing but a world of dew,
> And yet . . .
> And yet . . .

Later Issa resumed his journey. When he returned home again he wrote *Oraga Haru (The Year of My Life)*. In 1820 a son was born but died after four months. Two years later a third son was born. The next year Kiku died in May and the boy in December. On November 19, 1827, Issa himself died. He was sixty-four. Did he regret the bonds of human love that produced the pain coming with the loss of his four children? No. One autumn he wrote:

> In my secret heart
> I give thanks to my children
> As the night grows cold.

At times I feel as if I am stumbling down a path where Issa once walked. As a poet or spiritual seeker there can be no comparison. But he was also a father to a little girl. When we were both nearing sixty we lived under the shadow of a killer virus. And we both walked with a child into the heart of God.

Issa had a keen spiritual awareness. He knew there would have to be a special year in his life after the death of Sato. I was to have an unparalleled year after Tina's death, but I was not aware of the year or even the need for it until later. That seems to be the way it happens to many, if not most, of us. The German poet Rainer Marie Rilke wrote:

> *And you suddenly know: It was here!*
> *You pull yourself together, and there*
> *stands an irrevocable year*
> *of anguish and vision and prayer.*

In German the last line is *"Angst und Gestalt und Gebet." Angst*, a dreadful feeling of deep anxiety, controlled my life until it came in balance with prayer—*Gebet*. The teetertotter between pain and hope is a kind of vision. *Gestalt* has also come to mean comprehending a fundamental wholeness in life. When Tina died I could no longer repress my grief for all the beauty and innocence I had seen destroyed in six decades of living on this planet. Nor could I any longer deny that I had often contributed to that profanation.

5

Y ou shall know the truth," wrote Flannery
O'Connor, "and the truth shall make you
odd." In my fifty-ninth year, a year before Tina
died, I learned some deeply troubling facts
about what it means to live in this age. This
knowledge did indeed contribute to my odd-
ness.

December 1989 had been an exuberant time
for the world. Freedom was sweeping over
Central and Eastern Europe. For forty-four
years the individual liberties of peoples had
been suppressed for the theoretical dream of an
unattainable millennium. Communism was a
system having one answer to all questions. But
by the 1980s even the omnipotent answer was
forgotten, and the struggle had evolved into
the ancient conflict between "the state" and "the
people." It was, and always has been, a question
of power. Who will be master and who will be
servant? By 1989 women and men of the Soviet
Bloc were overcoming their fear and were saying "This is enough." When communism became a moral issue, the system tumbled.

The revolution was actually a reformation, a return to prized and almost forgotten values. There was little conflict in the final stages of change. Communism was defeated as if by the will of the oppressed. In most places there was little bloodshed. In what was then Czechoslovakia, the revolt was labeled "the Velvet Revolution." Then came Romania—an hour of disbelief, a minute of euphoria, days of violence. In the bloody upheaval, doors were opened on a few of the dark areas in that tragic country. One of those doors revealed the faces of children with AIDS.

In 1990 there were over 120,000 abandoned children in Romania still alive. Many of them were handicapped. Thousands also had AIDS. Most lived in subhuman conditions because many of the people who knew of the situation did not consider these orphans human. There has been a continuing struggle in this century to extend the definition of "human being" to the poor, the handicapped, the very young. In 1990 it had not been extended to the suffering children of Romania.

For decades 23 million oppressed Romanians hungered for freedom and for food. Two priorities for Nicolae Ceauşescu, Romania's tyrant, were to build a bigger workforce by increasing the population and to obtain funds by exporting most of the food produced. This was an absurd combination of policies. Parents were forced to have children they could not feed. Pregnancy inspectors regularly visited the workplace. Birth control was prohibited. In 1966 abortion was outlawed for any woman, even very young rape victims, who had not delivered four children. Many of the handicapped orphans were the result of desperate attempts at self-abortion. Increasingly sickly children were taken to hospitals by parents who never returned for them.

Ceauşescu was Romania's absolute ruler. He was also mentally unbalanced. These qualities made him attractive to Washington. Our leaders encouraged him to become a loose cannon in the Soviet Bloc. Ceauşescu fell in love with western buildings. He was embarrassed by the peasant class from which he came and had seven thousand peasant villages bulldozed. High-rise apartment buildings were thrown up in which elevators and plumbing seldom worked. When housing was at its worst, he began construction on a one thousand-room palace that cost billions. At one time twenty thousand people were working on it. For all these plans this deranged pharaoh needed a large workforce.

Ceauşescu also needed hard western currency for his projects. He sold everything—even children. The orphanages were divided into four categories: healthy children, slightly handicapped, handicapped, and "irrecuperables." Healthy children were treated fairly well. They had beds and food. Many were adopted by eager couples in France, Italy, Germany, and the United States for high prices. Leftover boys were often trained for the Securitate, Ceauşescu's large and feared secret police. The lot of the "irrecuperables" was different. They were fed and housed like animals: no beds, no diapers, food in a common dish on the ground.

AIDS likely entered Romania through Constanţa, the nation's ancient Black Sea port. Sailors, both foreign and domestic, supplemented their meager wages with blood donations. Until 1990 blood was seldom tested for HIV, the virus which causes AIDS. One of the uses for a unit of blood was an archaic practice of transfusing sickly newborns through the umbilical cord. One unit of HIV infected blood would service several babies. The virus then was

24

spread to other children by the practice of using one needle to inoculate a number of children in an institution. In 1990 almost a third of the institutionalized children in the Constanța district were found to be infected with the HIV virus.

Eastern Romania's first children with AIDS were hidden in dark rooms until they died. Doctors concerned about the crisis were warned they would be jailed if they continued their investigation. Ceaușescu decreed there was no AIDS in Romania. But Ceaușescu and his wife were executed on Christmas Day 1989. Then the children came into the light.

6

The world was shocked at the faces of Romania's neglected children. I was to become a small facet of that outrage. One evening, on a television news program, I saw pictures of an emaciated Romanian child with AIDS. I was shaken by the sight. It was her eyes, I had never before seen such deep fear in the eyes of any being. Something snapped inside me and I announced I was going to Romania. Julie and Marti were amazed because they had trouble getting me to take the two-hour trip from the farm to Santa Rosa, the county seat.

Why did I go? Perhaps it had something to do with Tina. We were going to lose her. I would not say it. I would not want to think it. But at some deep level I knew she was dying. I could not help her. This lovely little girl was suffering and there was nothing I could do about it. I felt so angry, helpless, and sad. When I heard about Romania's children with AIDS, I was in no mood to excuse the indifference of the authorities. So like some slightly ridiculous medieval character, I went forth to battle dragons in the name of my little princess.

On my first visit to Romania I attempted to find the infected children. That is how I came to the city of Cernavoda, a short distance inland from the port of Constanța.

Cement factories crowd the banks of the great Danube River where once could be found little farms. The product of these factories goes to build a gigantic nuclear power plant whose massive stacks rise eerily into the sky. Behind these towering structures is a hill. On the hill, slightly above the tops of the chimneys, is a building in which Romanian authorities had warehoused some children. The facility was almost hidden by trees and neighboring buildings. It looked old. There was a playground that had not been used in a long time. Grass grew tall under the empty and rusting swings. I opened the door. It creaked. The ominous hall was long, leading to nowhere. When I finally encountered someone in white, I was motioned to an office. The director shook hands perfunctorily and gave me over to Ioana, a worried head nurse. We started out. There were more long halls and many rooms in this place. I went to wash my hands so as not to bring any alien germs into the wards. There was no disinfectant and no soap near the basin. No hot water came from the tap. Ioana shrugged sadly. Slowly I looked around. The children all had shaved heads. "No lice medicine," she explained. It was not possible to distinguish boys from girls. Many children had eye infections. The cribs were without mattresses, only rags stuffed in sacks. There were no diapers other than a tucked-in loincloth. All the children I picked up were wet, as were their beds.

Many of the attendants had hard faces. They stood back from the children. It was obvious they did not want to touch them. I saw a nurse carrying a child—holding him out at arm's length! Later I discovered that some of the staff were there as a condition of parole from prison.

There was a pervasive unpleasant smell. It seemed to be strongest near the windows. Perhaps it came up from the construction on the nuclear power plant. The walls of the rooms were a sickly green. Rust was common on the metal cribs. I doubt if anyone worried about lead poisoning. The crib sides were of heavy mesh resembling cyclone fences. In one room a dozen toddlers wandered about. They appeared disoriented. A few toys were on the floor. Pictures were hung too high for the children to see. The only child who seemed at home was emotionally disturbed. At least he was content.

This was an unhappy place. Everybody wanted out. The children wanted out. The staff wanted out. I wanted out! There are some facilities that are just very bad places. This was one of them.

Dazed, I moved from room to room. In one, a child greeted me as I entered. She may have been a new arrival who still had hope of being picked up. I obliged. She collapsed on my shoulder. Tears came to my eyes. She reminded me of Tina, who also would melt her body into mine in utter confidence. The weight of this little girl was the same as Tina's and so holding her was a familiar sensation. But Tina was two and this child was almost four. I was dismayed to even consider that a child in our family could have ended up in a place like this. The little girl in my arms deserved to be in someone's family. She was a human being. I wanted to shout it out, "She's a human being!" Sadly, I put her back in her crib. Would I ever see her again? My God, what I would have given to walk out of there with her. With them all.

I walked into a big room with no children. A small door at the other end was open. I assumed it was probably a closet but I looked anyway. It was no closet. Eight cribs were crammed into this nook. Two shaved heads peaked over the bars. Six other boys and girls without hope or energy lay in the dim light. My fragile emotional shell cracked. I wanted to tear down this hell hole stone by stone. A flood of pain and sorrow mixed with my anger. Tears filled my eyes. I turned back to the doorway and exploded at the staff in the other room. Some looked worried. One cried with me.

I will always see the bars of that room. Bars, and children behind bars, and little hands on bars, some with souls screaming to get out, others quietly extinguishing the flames and going into their own world.

When I could control my emotions, I returned to the room and made contact with each child. Some could respond. Some could not. As I left the children in the eight cribs, I knew this would always be for me "The Room." I would be able to see it vividly for the rest of my life. I do not believe I had really understood the possibilities of human callousness until I entered that room. I did not want to go on exploring that pit. I really wanted to get away from the building. It was a place of no movement. The children were not placed there for medical reasons. They were quarantined. There was no treatment. In most cases there were no symptoms. Those who were sinking were getting sicker from the place. No one was getting better. No one was experiencing anything of life. They were just in a waiting room, waiting for nothing.

Walking down the hall I realized I had seen no shoes. On a floor with over fifty three- and four-year-olds there were no shoes anywhere. No one in there was ever intended to go outside to that silent playground, or anywhere else.

I asked Ioana the name of the place. "House of Children," she said. It should have been called "House of Tears."

In one of the many gray halls Ioana introduced me to Laura. She was interested in the development of the children. We walked together to a broad stairwell where we could talk. Laura's animated and concerned countenance was a relief from the unsympathetic faces of the other adults in the wards.

"Have they found the cure for the virus yet?" Laura asked. I shook my head. "Is there any hope? Is anybody doing anything?" My response was complex and brought little comfort. She spoke through tears. "The little coffins. The children are so thin, so sad, as they lie there. We are forsaken. God has forgotten us!" I reached out to her but she ran up the stairs in distress. What could I have said to her anyway? Have things really changed since the first infected children were hidden here in a dark room? Were not most of the people I met still standing around waiting for these children to die? This institution, with its inhuman conditions, is hidden from the world. "God has forgotten us" is a reasonable conclusion for the few who care. No words will reassure Laura. Only deeds. People would have to become the hands of God. We could not forget these children. A world that would let these children go by was not going to be a world I could live in.

Later that evening I sat in my hotel room looking out over the Black Sea. Suddenly the dark of the night gave way to sheets of lightning. Out my window I could see for miles out to sea. A long time later came the thunder. Flash followed on flash. Light and dark were equal. Now all was black. The next minute I saw the beach and waves. The rage of the electrical storm was strangely comforting to me. I was also full of rage and troubled. It was hard to leave children in such a deplorable state. I had known I would see bad conditions, but I did not realize I would have to handle my own strong emotions at simply walking away. Doing so was a betrayal.

Picking up my prayer book, I turned to the readings assigned for Vespers on that day. My eyes fell on the antiphon verse. I was startled at what I saw.

I will not leave you orphans; I am going now but I will come back to you and your hearts will rejoice.

The faces of the children in the wards rushed into my mind. Hot tears came up again. "God will find a way," I screamed out. "You are not forgotten."

7

On many dark and fearful nights the souls of Romania's children with AIDS must have screamed into the unknown. Did heaven react? I believe so. It is arrogant to believe I had a personal call from God to do something in Romania. But if I was somehow part of God's response, I know whose prayer was being answered.

Dana Rica and I first met in an AIDS ward at Constanţa's Municipal Hospital. There were sixty children with AIDS in several wards on the third floor. Some were sick. A few were dying. Most had no other place to go and were sinking into darkness because of lack of nurturing. Few of the children made any sounds. But when I stepped into one ward I heard a laugh coming from a crib in the corner. It was the only sound in the room. In the crib I discovered a tiny girl with a smile. She was a beauty, even with her shaved head. Her dark eyes sparkled. I picked her up. She was wet. "What is her name?" I asked. The nurse asked an assistant, who had to ask another assistant.

No one really knew her name. No one cared.

Although she was two she weighed less than ten pounds and could not stand or sit up. I carried her around the room with me. She was very curious about the other children. It may have been the first time she had seen what was happening in the other cribs. Occasionally she would giggle at a child as I made contact with my free hand. The other children enjoyed her attention. After about fifteen minutes I felt I must go on to wards across the hall. As I started to put her down, she grabbed the cross I wear around my neck. I straightened up. She laid her head on my shoulder and we slowly made the rounds again. This time several children smiled at her. Once again I attempted to put her down. She cried and my heart broke. Tears filled my eyes. I held her tight and felt her small hand on my neck. We stood together until my eyes cleared. I laid her down. She turned to the wall.

Later I ascertained that her name was Dana Rica. There was a resonance to the name and to the child. When I returned to California, something of Dana Rica's spirit came with me. I was truly haunted by the sight of her lying in that cage. She was often in my dreams.

It was three months before my next trip to Constanţa. I assumed Dana Rica was dead. But I found her in the same ward. It was hard to recognize her. She was much thinner and very weak. I looked at her and asked, "Is it you?" She gazed up at me for a long time, then gave me a lovely smile. As I picked her up she went limp in my arms. Holding her unconscious body, I wondered if she had been waiting to die in the arms of someone who cared. After a while she came around. This was not to be the end of Dana Rica's adventure on the planet. What a waste these months had been. She could have known love. That day she was very tired. I put her down and stood for a long time watching over her as she slept.

I went home a wild man. Rationally I knew Dana Rica might have only a few weeks of life left. But there was still an opportunity to do something for one little girl. Julie was completely occupied with Tina's needs. But Marti steadily put aside her other work to lend a hand. She activated a moral steam roller that assaulted politicians, doctors, diplomats, journalists.

A senior producer at ABC-TV had followed our activities for years and now sensed that a story was unfolding. His crew followed Marti to Washington, D.C., and me to Romania. I welcomed the media. It gave me much-needed extra clout with the Romanian authorities. Turning a public spotlight on the plight of the children did more to improve their condition than any amount of moral reasoning. Surprisingly, the spotlight was also falling, uncomfortably, on me. Sometimes I was packaged as a saint when a reporter needed a saint. More often, and closer to the truth, I was presented as an offbeat character with whom people could identify. Segments appeared on national television entitled "Toby's Journey," "Toby's Kids," "Toby's Dream." For a few months I was a minor celebrity. That was a strain because I did not know how to let the media into my life or to respond to the public attention without trivializing the urgency I felt to get something real accomplished. The media and the public demand a high price for their attention. People in the limelight surrender privacy and are forced to handle other people's expectations. But I wanted to use the media interest without paying the price. For a while I got my own way.

With a TV camera constantly behind me, I

took uncharacteristic risks in negotiations with the Romanian authorities. Every gamble worked. It was not hard to believe that I was running to keep step with a God who was tired of being mocked.

Because of the publicity, volunteers came to our farm to be trained on the model of our family and then go to Romania. Many had paradoxical motives and were not appropriate. Some were awe-inspiring in their selfless love and dedication. One of these was Susan Walsh Belfiore, who was to become the most important person in Dana Rica's life. I pushed the coworkers hard. They accepted it.

The plan was to get the Romanian government to give the use of a suitable building and to convert it into foster-family units for five children each. We wanted to have at least thirty children to demonstrate an alternative to the way the children were being cared for. Romanian officials were unsure of themselves. There was a considerable amount of confusion and stress at every turn. The future was uncertain but I felt we had to be ready to move quickly to take advantage of any opportunity that might open up. Realistically, we doubted we could begin the first foster family until the spring of the next year. Now we must prepare and wait.

Autumn has always been my favorite time of year. But in 1990 it was to be a wild emotional storm. Tina was failing at home. Dana Rica was suffering in the squalor of a Romanian ward. Sleepless nights and constant worry made me remote from those I loved. My spiritual life was more a memory than a reality. The media was too close to painful situations I wanted to keep private. Yet I needed them. People with self-serving agendas were forever pushing themselves into my life, but I had to remain open to encourage those few others who really could help the children. I did not know how to find a balance. My normal defenses were crumbling. And I had forgotten how to turn to God.

8

By summer's end the herpes zoster virus had leapt through the breach in Tina's immune system. For most people the virus causes chickenpox and then lies dormant. Sometimes years later it may activate again as painful shingles. On Tina's body small pimples would grow to gaping ulcers. The first sight of these lesions caused several people to leave the room from shock. The medical regimen grew more complex and life more difficult.

Living with AIDS is learning to stumble backward over milestones without being destroyed. There are times when a person can no longer walk or talk or eat as once she or he could. Children with AIDS adapt to these losses better than those around them. There are also all the complicated medications, the hospitalizations, the doctors, and the occasional scream to remind well-meaning people of the human being behind the chart and at the end of the tubes. Children who are secure and bonded can cope even with all this. Tina did very well but she had her limits.

Julie worked hard to give Tina a good life and to keep her at home in the family she loved. However, the strain on Julie was increasing. She learned more skills, slept less, shared Tina's pain, and looked with sorrow into the future. Julie was sustained by Tina's delightful personality. Mother and daughter lived one day at a time and every moment to the fullest. For Tina there was no clear difference between her own person and Julie. As long as Julie could do things, Tina was functioning. If there was a party on a day when Tina could not digest food, she would simply feed ice cream to Julie. It was the same thing to Tina. I worried about what would happen to Julie when the time came that the bond was broken.

Thanksgiving was a hard day. We had been hoping for a much-needed respite from care, but Tina was limp and uncomfortable. Yet she insisted on being at the events of the day. Julie held her at the table for the Thanksgiving dinner. When Tina went into a deep slumber, the tears started rolling down Julie's cheeks and onto Tina's soft hair. Julie was truly washing her daughter with tears. We all knew that the best thing for both mother and child was to keep the meal and the day as normal as possible. We tried.

In early December Tina had to be hospitalized in San Francisco for unrelenting AIDS-related infections. Julie was with her. We felt the separation keenly because it was a four-hour drive from our home. Tina and Julie came home the week before Christmas. We have elaborate holiday traditions, which the children were old enough to expect. Everything is designed to culminate on Christmas Eve. But the night of peace we anticipated became a night of dread. On the twenty-third Tina had to be rushed to a hospital in Santa Rosa. We were advised she might not make it. Three years before, Josh, another child with AIDS in our home, had died on December 23.

The hospital was a two-hour drive away. Marti went with Tina and Julie. Tina's condition did not improve the next day. With the help of two friends I went through all the little moments that made Christmas Eve special to the other children. Marti and Julie were at the hospital with decreasing hopes. At the time in the evening when I took the children up the hill to the chapel, Marti and Julie were on either side of Tina's bed reciting the same songs and prayers. Afterward, as Tina slept, they drank a Christmas Eve toast from the little cups in Tina's favorite tea set.

Miraculously Tina started to improve on Christmas Day. When I was told the hospital was arranging a special visit from Santa, I told them it would not be necessary. After dressing quickly in our old Santa suit, I made the drive to the hospital in record time to be rewarded by the sight of Tina's watchful face framed in the small window in the door to her room.

Soon we were all together at home. Tina hung her stocking and we had another "Christmas Eve." In the days that followed Tina was comfortable but weak. She often wanted to be held and rocked. I liked to be the person holding her. One afternoon, while rocking back and forth, I realized what I had missed most from this Christmas season were the quiet times of sitting around and singing carols. I started to sing. It pleased Tina. She was practically purring. Song followed song. I was at every Christmas in my life. I was every person who had ever sung those songs. She was not a sick child and I was not an aging senior. We were father and daughter playing in the eye of the holiness and magic of Christmas. For the first time in months I felt at home.

I wanted no other life than what I was experiencing, good and bad, in my family. But there was another child calling me from a wretched hospital ward thousands of miles from Tina's tender realm.

9

Between Thanksgiving and Christmas, as Tina was being assaulted with so many hardships, an opportunity had begun to unfold in Romania.

Officially, local authorities were assuming we would not start caring for children until after Easter in 1991. There was still no firm assurance they really intended to cooperate with us. The shake of the head, the shrug, the explanation that "It is not possible" was the stylized response to almost every request we made. However, just before Christmas of 1990, through the help of Rodica Mătuşa, a caring and supportive physician at Constanţa's Municipal Hospital who had visited with us in Sonoma County, we negotiated to obtain an unused floor in a sanatarium. We were warned it would take a long time to make the space usable. I was told that we could start working out the practical details of the arrangement in a couple of months.

Romanians were preparing to celebrate their first Christmas holiday in decades. All officials in Constanţa would be gone for an important two weeks. Marti and I saw an opportunity and decided to follow an American military adage that it is sometimes "better to ask forgiveness than permission." One of our volunteers, Chuck Williams, went to Romania just before Christmas. Chuck, a devout Baptist from Alabama, can be stubborn. He was resolved to quickly construct apartments where our foster families could live. And to ignore anyone who told him it was impossible.

January 4, 1991, was my sixtieth birthday. I received a welcome telex that day. First, Dana Rica was still alive. Second, we were in possession of the floor. Chuck had moved in and was converting it into apartments. The first one would be ready in two weeks. Five more were planned.

It was time to move. But what about Tina?

"Go," said Julie. "We will be all right." Tina seemed to improve a little.

It was early morning when we left for the airport. I had said my good-bye to Tina in her room. But just as I was getting in the car, I saw Julie had carried Tina out on the lawn to wave good-bye. I went over for a hug. Survival was a struggle for her. I did not want to leave her. My place was with her. But my place was also with Dana Rica in Romania. That moment was the first time I felt two little girls meet in my heart. Tina smiled and pointed to the car. I left. She waved.

We arrived in a crippled Romania. The January weather was fierce. My hotel room had a broken window and heating was nonexistent. A trickle of lukewarm water could be obtained for only a short time each day. Coats and hats were worn in the restaurant. There was no menu. Sometimes there was no food. Always a somber band played off-key. "Goldfinger," from a James Bond movie, was a favorite piece. Rooms were dark because the staff would steal the scarce light bulbs. Theft was a part of daily life.

On the morning after our arrival we were told a senior health official believed all children with AIDS should remain in medical institutions. Also, an "expert" who had drawn up an agreement between us and the local government was out of town. We would have to wait for his return. We did not. At that time Romanian bureaucrats did not know what to do when someone refused to accept a no. I wrote an amendment responding to the official's concerns and within an hour we were in his office.

The medical establishment of Constanța had gathered to look on. An ABC-TV camera was rolling as the conference began. The chief health officer was sizing us up. We passed. "Welcome to Constanța," he proclaimed. Everyone applauded. He and I embraced. All was cleared to begin the next morning.

I slept little. Having the children liberated from their cages and placed in Susan's arms would be a dream fulfilled. Before dawn I called Susan at the new apartment. She had been up for some time making the place nice. "It feels like Christmas morning," she bubbled. I heard soft music playing in the background. We agreed to meet at eight.

I rearranged the pillow I had stuffed in the broken window. It was snowing heavily outside. Wrapped in blankets, I prayed. My thoughts went back to the warm chapel at home and a little girl waving good-bye. "Bittersweet" is a term I heard the TV people using often. This day, January 17, would be "bittersweet."

There was a knock at the door. A solemn TV producer stood in the dark hallway. "I thought you would want to know," she said, "we are bombing Iraq. There have been one thousand strikes. The war has begun."

As I moved through the day I usually had a Romanian child in my arms. And in my mind was the image of Tina thousands of miles away. I also imagined children frightened, suffering, dying as the bombs fell on Iraq. Here we were, a small group of Americans, fighting to give a few children the chance to experience life while American planes were killing people in the next time zone. It was a paradox that profoundly troubled me.

The local health authorities became invested in making our experiment work. Consequently they suggested that we take only the healthier children. They were especially concerned about Dana Rica. "She will give you much trouble and be dead soon," I was warned. "It must be," I insisted. They acquiesced.

There were many conferences, handshakes, and hollow laughs. But at last the moment came when we began taking the children out of wards. Dana Rica was asleep and not the first to come.

The transformations were instantaneous. I tried hard not to look surprised. It was all turning out better than we had predicted. Subdued, pathetic victims were becoming curious and playful little girls and boys before our eyes. A

49

few Romanians watching from a distance began to cry.

At last Dana Rica's turn came. I leaned over the crib. She smiled. I had the strong feeling she knew what was happening. I picked her up and we walked slowly out of the ward. She played with my beard and touched my eyes. There was a deep silence when we went into the apartment. Susan embraced both of us. We stood together as I recited the dedication we use for the children at Starcross.

> O gentle God,
> here is your child, and our daughter.
> Touch her with your spirit,
> put your star within her heart.
> Help her to walk with you
> all the days of her life.

Then she was taken out of my arms and her hospital rags thrown away. A bath, which she much enjoyed, was followed by considerable attention to her coming-out attire. A pretty little pixie emerged ready to meet her new family.

Dana Rica was two but she weighed less than most one-year-olds. She looked delicate and could not walk. We were concerned about how she would survive the roughhousing of older and more active siblings. She crawled out to the middle of the floor. The biggest boy promptly sat on her head. We were terrified, until we heard a thin sound. Dana Rica was laughing!

The children knew how to be children. All they wanted from us was a chance to live.

10

Susan needed the next day to be alone with her new family. I attempted to run away from AIDS for a while by visiting Medgidia, Dana Rica's birthplace. I wanted to know what life was like for Romanian children who were not infected with AIDS or abandoned in institutions.

The early-morning sky was clear in Medgidia. Sunshine reflected off the packed snow in the streets. An icy wind blew across the canal and into the open space where the market should be. But there was little to sell. A long line waited for the bread truck to arrive. On the canal a large and colorful family of gypsies boarded the ferry to the railway station.

Children were coming from every direction. I thought of the children who were not on the streets. Hundreds of Medgidia's children had already died because of AIDS and bad care. Many were waiting for death in hellish places. At least one was playing with Susan that morning. I wondered how many families I saw on the streets had taken a child with AIDS to the hospital and then returned months later with a little coffin.

On a bright day in a street filled with children I was thinking of coffins! It seemed as if I could not escape AIDS. It was eating at children I loved and, in the process, destroying my ability to respond to life.

Being the only foreigner, I soon collected a crowd of curious children. They were well wrapped against the cold. Most were wearing everything they owned. The youngest, about six, showed only her bright eyes to the world. I was reminded of those sets of roly-poly Ukrainian dolls nestled inside each other. Our children at home were fascinated by these dolls within a doll within a doll. Sometimes ten dolls were fitted inside each other. Perhaps our psyches are constructed in the same fashion. Within two-year-old Dana Rica there is the baby she was and the eight-year-old she may never become. If so, there is also the twenty-year-old and the eighty-year-old. Around me that cold morning were children who perhaps had within them many other psyches including those of the hundreds of Medgidia's children who will never walk its streets.

The clanging of a bell drew attention to a

small herd of sheep and goats. They trotted down the main street, with a frustrated shepherd running after them. We all laughed and for a little while I was distracted from my cheerless thoughts.

With the help of a translator I talked to my small flock. We spoke of school, looked at books, seriously depleted the stock of the town's one sweet shop, walked and joked. I wondered if someday these children would learn of the hundreds who were born in this town but lived and died in dark and friendless places. I wondered if they would care.

The morning passed. Parents were preparing the main, and in some homes the only, meal of the day. We said good-bye and I walked toward the car. A thirteen-year-old came with me. We talked of things that filled his days. As I stepped into the car I asked, "What will you be doing when you are sixteen?" Without hesitation he responded, "Whatever I can do." That was also the goal of a little two-year-old from Medgidia who was just learning to play—and to live.

In the months that followed there would be many miracles for Dana Rica and those who loved her. Susan learned she had trouble eating. The first meals were very slow. No one had been willing to help her that much before. Her weight would double in a short time. The emaciated waif would be replaced by a chubby cherub. She would grow beautiful hair and love her new shoes. She would clap wildly when she liked something. And, despite medical opinion to the contrary, she would learn to walk and talk.

I called home in the evening. We had a bad connection. Tina was weak. It was disappointing. Apparently I had been hoping for an improvement. As I watched Dana Rica and her new brothers and sisters begin a new life, it was hard to accept that Tina was also not going to benefit by some absurd cosmic windfall.

Marti and Julie were sickened by what was happening in the Persian Gulf War. Incredible firepower was being used. There had to be heavy civilian casualties. On this topic the media was quiet. The Pentagon assured the country that all air strikes were "surgical." There was strong public support for the war and no one wanted to hear about dead civilians.

The next day I played with all the kids in the new family most of the morning. My thoughts were often on Tina. At naptime Dana

Rica preferred my arms to her bed. It pleased me greatly. I sang the songs I sang at home for Tina. Dana Rica peacefully rested her little head on my shoulder. All she needed at that moment was a shoulder, and in the silence I could be myself. I felt very tired. Heavy. Wasted. Old.

Slowly I realized my work was finished. Not just the task of being true to this little girl, but also all my humanitarian agendas. There was no unfinished business. A more radical venture was beginning. The advice coming from the shadows of my consciousness said "Go home to Starcross, be with Tina, love the children at your hearth, look into your soul, look for God in little things."

I thought Dana Rica was asleep and I moved to her crib. As I was putting her down, she took hold of the side and stood up. She smiled and waved. It reminded me of Tina's wave, which had been like a blessing and a command the day I left California. I knew it was time to leave Dana Rica. But I also knew she would be with me as I sat with Tina.

11

It was good to be home. Because of the seriousness of Tina's needs, the family had settled into orbit around her. This was where I longed to be. It was easy to say no to requests and tasks that would have taken me from the family circle. Without my usual distractions I more easily became aware of the presence of God in every minute of our day.

The week before Easter our old apple trees burst into bloom. During the Palm Sunday service Tina was mostly asleep in Julie's arms. But once, when we were all standing around the altar, I turned to find Tina beside me solemnly holding out a small palm cross for me to take. In this final gift was all the peace of our hours of rocking, singing, making up stories, and looking at little things.

Despite our sorrow Holy Week was a time of deep peace. The days were filled with the beauty of nature and the sounds of children. Every morning five-year-old David would play his violin for Tina. It soothed her. Her message to us was that everything should be normal.

Midweek we gathered for a ritual meal. Tina insisted on having one-year-old Holly beside her. She carefully looked after Holly's needs. The next day I was going up the hill to the chapel on our all-terrain vehicle. Tina let me know she wanted to sit in front of me and hold on to the handlebars, as she had so often done in better times. We were apprehensive but up the hill she went.

On Holy Saturday, the day before Easter, Julie gathered Marti and me for a sad session. It was hard for her to say the words. Once they passed her lips, our lives would be forever changed. It was, she said, time to let go. Tina was ready and we must prepare. Julie chose a site for the grave and gave instructions for a homemade coffin. Marti made the necessary calls. Then we turned our full attention to Tina and the family.

We went about the tasks of preparing for Easter Sunday. Sometimes sobs from deep within would escape. It hurt so very much.

Easter was a beautiful day. I still find that incredible. Like all the children, Tina was dressed up when she went to the chapel. Julie sat in a rocker holding her. Little Holly played with her Easter basket at Julie's feet. Tina watched. At the center of the chapel was our Paschal candle. It is a symbol of Jesus' message that death is not the final word. We decorate our own candles. This year we used symbols of faith, hope, and love topped with a rainbow. Julie put one little bluebird above the rainbow. We knew this represented our Tina and all the other Tinas in the world.

The week after Easter was gentle. Tina liked to be in her bed or sleeping with Julie. She wanted her family near.

On April the ninth, a little past midday, Tina died in her mother's arms. As with Sato, it was the hour when the morning glories closed their petals.

I choked as I cried out to her. My little daughter had completed a race. She had crossed the finish line. I was a proud parent cheering from the stand. I was a lonely daddy torn apart with grief.

We sang. We prayed. We talked to Tina. Julie wrapped Tina and carried her to the chapel. Marti and I were on either side. It was a slow and peaceful procession. Our little girl was gone. And yet she was with us. So was

God in a calm and constant way I had never before experienced. That day I learned the meaning of "grace."

The naturalness of Tina's death was profound. There were no great jarring episodes. The private funeral Mass, which I had dreaded, was an organic outflowing of healing mercy. We gathered in the chapel Tina loved and we did what we normally did. David played his violin for her as he had every morning. The little open coffin was part of the circle we made around the altar. At a point where we ordinarily join hands, the persons on either side of the coffin, without hesitation, reached for the familiar little hands. The circle was complete.

The coffin was closed and carried to the nearby grave by loving hands. On each corner was a person who had played with Tina and cared for her. One was her dedicated physician, Frank Miraglia, who had treated her as he would have his own daughter. When the service ended Julie experienced a wrenching emptiness and sorrow. For a long time she knelt beside the grave. It was then that she first heard a voice inside using the familiar ritual words she so often used to comfort Tina: "You're

doing fine. Everything is going to be okay."
Julie stood up and we moved away.

We walked back to the house past the last
apple blossoms of spring. The previous Easter
I had held Tina up to smell the blooms on those
old trees. Without warning another strong
memory from that happier time pushed into my
mind. A year ago Julie had that dream about a
blue whale named Philip. I remembered Julie's
words at the end:

> If my baby can be with him, deep in the
> ocean, underneath the stars, it will be all
> right. I can be there too. We can all be there
> together.

The week following Tina's death is befogged
in my memory. There were many private moments of deep grieving. My lamentations were
for the loss of Tina and every other slaughter
of the pure and innocent I had witnessed during
my sixty years. I cried for every unfulfilled
dream.

Despite the tears, the incredible feeling of
naturalness continued. Toward the end of the
month we had a public gathering. Press and
television people were present. Those in at-

tendance did a number of good things together, but we were there for one primary task. Julie had written in the invitation:

> Tina was pure and unbounded joy. When she finished singing a song she would clap and say "Yea, Tina!" After courageously enduring some treatment we would say to her "Yea, Tina!" She would smile and clap. Looking at her whole life, which was a great life, I want everyone who knew her to clap and say "Yea, Tina!"

The time came. We all stood and held each other as "Yea, Tina!" rolled from every mouth. The clapping went on and on in a wave that crashed over the walls of the room and splashed into the cosmos. The echo of that moment will resound forever in my soul.

At the end of the service Tina's friends went back into their lives. Most assumed I would do the same. Only Julie and Marti knew that I would never again travel the path I had walked a few months before. I stepped back onto another road—a deeply quiet way I had been experiencing in the months when I was holding Tina. Rationally, children and the contemplative life may not seem to go together. I have learned that they do. In *Oraga Haru* Issa quotes the Zen poet Basho:

> *Not having experienced love*
> *For your children,*
> *There is no wisdom for cherry blossoms.*

With love for my children in my heart, I was ready for blossoms.

12

We made a difference in Romania. But my contribution was largely in storming the battlements. For over a year I played hardball with Romanian bureaucrats. The games were often on a base level. I learned when to smile and when to push. The interest of the American media brought useful pressure on disinterested officials. Power was what the Romanian establishment respected, and a mystique of power grew around me. I used it, and at the same time it was eating up my soul. The chief AIDS physician in Constanţa referred to me as the "guardian angel of Constanţa's children." I wished the people of Romania saw themselves in that role. After a meeting at the Romanian Academy, the philosopher Mihai Drăgănescu leaned over the table and took my hand. "What you are doing," he said, "will light a flame in hearts that have forgotten people can make a difference in each other's lives." I wanted him to be right. But I had doubts.

My own spirit and health were being crushed as the months wore on. I hid this fact as best

I could. In the spring of 1991 welcome relief was available. Some remarkable women made the dream a reality, while I stumbled along to keep pace with them. Marti took over most of my administrative duties. Even in her grieving, Julie turned her attention to the needs of the individual children at our "Casa Speranţă" (House of Hope). Right after Tina died Marolen Mullinax became a volunteer foster mother and the supervisor at Casa Speranţă. In a way Tina had been Marolen's primary teacher while Marolen trained with our family at Starcross, and the lessons she learned were quickly put to the test in Romania. A Texan with a lot of grit and common sense, Marolen guided Casa Speranţă through continual crises until finally, after many months, everything began to work as we had dreamed.

Casa Speranţă housed thirty children. There were six families each with five children and a foster mother. The rusting metal cribs were thrown out. For the first time the kids ate from plates and drank from cups. They wore regular clothes and played outside. Beautiful hair grew and was brushed. Love and care encouraged them to give life another chance. Some we were told would never walk did walk. Children with "retarded" labels developed normally. Soon the children fed themselves and helped send all the bottles back to the hospital. Diapers became a thing of the past. The children's keen curiosity about life motivated Julie to work with our friend Rebecca Ault to establish a Montessori school at Casa Speranţă. It was the first in eastern Romania.

Miracles were a daily occurrence. Over two years after we began, every child was still alive. All the other children who had been patients at the hospital when we started were dead.

My experience with dying children in Romanian institutions is a nightmare. Shrunken, starving bodies encasing frightened souls. Even a gentle touch would bring forth an animal cry of despair. "They are not used to being touched," one embarrassed doctor explained to me. I vividly remember the first time I saw a dead child removed from the hospital wards. She or he had died in the night. The cleaning women put the body in a sack and carried it out with the morning garbage. I asked the child's name. They did not know. Dragos was the first child at Casa Speranţă to die. Everybody knew his name and will remember it.

Dragos had been limp when he came two years before. He was three years old and not expected to live more than a short time longer. Instead, he became an active and very independent little fellow who took great delight in his world. Dragos loved school. There were bouts of sickness, but he was quite secure and fearless. It was a wonderful two years for him.

Dragos died the week after Easter 1993. His last days were very peaceful. Those he knew and loved surrounded him. Like Issa's Sato and our Tina, Dragos died at midday—as the morning glories were closing. He died during naptime. It seemed natural. Familiar hands dressed him in his new Easter suit. There was an Orthodox service and he was buried with dignity.

Whether out of guilt, coercion, or a reawakened sense of conscience, children with AIDS in the worst-hit section of Romania were now being seen as human beings. A growing number of Romanians came to trust that we had no interest other than the well-being of the children.

We helped improve the quality of medical care. Strange practices were questioned. Romanian doctors were brought to the United

States for training. American physicians became long-distance consultants. There were regular donations of medicines.

Casa Speranță was yeast in the whole area. The sight of our happy children changed the attitude of the establishment toward other children with AIDS. More humane care was given in the institutions. Some families overcame their fear of AIDS and took their children back home. Health officials no longer insisted on removing infected children from their homes. A weekly clinic was opened to give support to families caring for their children with AIDS.

Romania is a hard place in which to make changes. Large organizations spent hundreds of thousands of dollars and often gave up in disgust and went home. Marti, Julie, and Marolen had only a few dollars, but they made sure we stayed—abandoning the children was not an option. And their resolve and success let me take off the oppressive armor I had worn for so long. However, I was beginning to think it was too late.

After Tina's death, and the stress of Romania, I was too tired to be a full-time warrior. I had to accept the other sides of my being. The frequently moody, melancholy, depressed, angry, buffeted, confused, self-pitying, injured fellow was also me. I became conscious of increasingly morbid thoughts. One day I was stunned to discover myself seriously considering suicide. I was sitting on a bench as the children played in the water. Objectively, it had been a good day. The lack of any specific problem is what made the situation so real. I had simply grown profoundly weary of life itself. To start another day would be an unwelcome struggle. I had been fighting with death for a long time over a child I loved. She was at peace. I was not. It felt as if I was on the frontier of my existence all day and night. I wanted to surrender to death. But, I did not. The new dawn came and I was there. Looking back now on the experience I am both frightened and resolute.

Five months after Tina died, the story of Dana Rica and her new home was aired on American television. The producer had known Tina. He had a picture of her on his computer. Unknown to me, he was emphasizing in the piece a connection between Tina and Dana

Rica. The segment was titled "Toby's Dream," and as one little face dissolved into another I saw my dream revealed. That night 17 million viewers understood that these little girls were sisters to each other and daughters to us all.

Something was completed. I could turn to the next step in my life.

13

Through the years I have encountered several references to "the song of the fisherman" in Chinese stories. Although the beginnings of the fables vary, the endings are always the same. A famous statesman is found on the riverbank by the emperor's envoys. They bring news of his appointment as prime minister. He interrupts the formalities with "Listen! The song of the fisherman," drawing attention to an ordinary man downstream.

There is a most ancient poem in which a poet laments that he alone is unsoiled and the world is dirty. A nearby fisherman rows away singing that he will wash his feet in the clean river water. When examined too closely, the whole thing gets fairly esoteric. But through the centuries many weary pilgrims have used the simple and wholesome song of the fisherman to mitigate the complexity of life. In the eighth century Wang Wei wrote:

In my later years I want only peace.
World affairs no longer excite my tired heart.

I return to my house in the woods.
The wind blows through the pines and frees my sash.
In the light of the mountain moon I play my lute.

You ask if I have formulated a philosophy
to explain having and not having.
Listen! The fisherman's song floats down the river.

Gradually I became calm enough occasionally to hear, very faintly, an almost forgotten song. It was a long process that had begun in the pain of Tina's death.

The month after Tina died, Julie and I went to Romania and then visited Assisi in northern Italy. As we said good-bye to the children and the volunteers in Romania, I was aware that I was very tired.

At some subconscious level I had probably been bargaining with the cosmos for months. My plea was to be excused from the struggles associated with AIDS in Romania. One morning in Assisi I was to find the beginning of an answer to my prayer.

The pilgrimage to the city of St. Francis was a remarkably peaceful time for two troubled souls. We stayed near the basilica dedicated to Francis's extraordinary disciple Clare, or

"Chiara" as she was known by her townspeople. Early on the first morning we walked to Santa Chiara to pray. The church's alternating layers of rose and white marble glistened in the soft morning light. By contrast the cavernous interior was dark and still. We were alone in the main part of the church for about half an hour. A few worshipers were gathering in a side chapel for Mass. We joined them. The room was well lighted, and I focused on the vibrant frescoes.

The sound of a priest's voice drew my attention. I turned toward the altar. There was no priest in sight. A woman sang a beautiful high-pitched response. A choir took up the lilting chant. They were nowhere to be seen. The nuns and their priest were on the other side of the wall behind the empty altar. Unseen, but heard, the ancient morning drama was unfolding as it had for over seven hundred years. Beside me sat Julie. Nearby were a few Hispanic sisters, two well-dressed Italian women, a businessman, a troubled-looking youth, a scholarly German, three poor and elderly local women. Silently we all faced the empty altar. The tones from the concealed priest and choir rolled on. This marginalized relationship to the ritual was oddly comforting. Relations with the institutional church have always been troublesome to me. Here in this motherhouse of one of the most traditional orders I would have expected to be struck by the differences that divided me from the nuns. Instead I was conscious of what bound us together. The wall between us was in fact a bridge.

Interiorly I was experiencing an almost constant jumble of wordy reflections and wordless flashes. Voices with words and voices without words were in unaccustomed and uncomfortable coexistence. The words, no matter how insightful or beloved, were tiring.

After Mass I went to an adjoining room to view the painted crucifix before which Francis had prayed. The icon originally hung in San Damiano, then a crumbling rural chapel. When Francis heard a voice say "Repair my church," he naively assumed it meant to rebuild the shrine. He set to work and in the process revitalized the whole church of his age. The nuns brought this treasure with them when they moved from San Damiano following Chiara's death in 1253. The icon's beauty lies in its ordinariness. A sober Jesus focuses on what can be seen only from the perspective of the cross. What he sees is troubling.

The crucifix hangs behind glass, which brought to mind Issa's image of the broken window.

> *How lovely it is*
> *to look through the broken window*
> *and discover the Milky Way.*

My world was broken. Was it Tina's death? The children in Romania? The loss of dreams? The cumulative effect of living in stress? I longed to see the Milky Way. In that quiet place, before the San Damiano crucifix, my wordless prayer went deep into divine nothingness. I felt free of the tattered places in which I so often related to politicians, media, physicians, and sometimes even people who meant the most to me in the world. For a long moment I had no specific goal other than to plunge into the mystery of God—to find rest. This was what I wanted. What stood in my way? Only me. Could I change my habits, live without the sense of romantic adventure, give up the skills I had learned, the praise I received, the power I could wield?

The blessed stillness was spoiled repeatedly by my restless thoughts. Lines from T. S. Eliot's "Little Gidding" came to mind.

> *We shall not cease from exploration*
> *And the end of all our exploring*
> *Will be to arrive where we started*
> *And know the place for the first time.*

Was that where I had at last come? To where I had started? Now, before this icon that had spoken to Francis, was I at last beginning to look beyond the broken window? Could I hope to find the Milky Way? What was required?

> *A condition of complete simplicity*
> *(Costing nothing less than everything)*
> *And all shall be well and*
> *All manner of thing shall be well.*

Eliot had used the words of Julian of Norwich. They reminded me that Julie was with me. At first I did not see her for she was in the pew behind me. She touched my shoulder. I must have seemed a bit disoriented. "You have been here quite a while," she said. "Would you like to go outside in the sunlight?" I stood up.

We walked back into the dark nave and toward the entrance. An afterimage of the crucifix was in my mind as well as the phrase "complete simplicity."

Living is a complex process. The ways we relate to each other are increasingly superficial. The problems we face are progressively more profound. Have we recently made some fundamental miscalculations about what it means to be human? I want to separate myself from the crowd and retrace history's steps a bit, searching for simplicity. This is not an attempt to find a protective niche from adversity. There is no personal exemption from the pain of this age. AIDS. Wars. Terrorism. Famine. Destruction of nature. Drugs. Violence. Homelessness. Anxiety. Fear. The empty sense of self. The lust for power. Dishonesty. Manipulation. Cynicism. Mistrust. These are the sick and unavoidable realities in my world. But there is more to existence.

For years I have concentrated too much on cracks. Now I want to look through the broken window, to include in my experience not only the tattered world but also the Milky Way. I have an intense longing to comprehend the whole human experience. To do this I must find the God who dwells in the life I share with my neighbors on this planet.

One warm afternoon in Assisi Julie and I visited Francis's forest hermitage. It is a short distance outside the walls of Assisi on Monte Subasio. Eremo Delle Carceri, "the hermitage of the cells," is a random collection of small stone buildings. There was obviously no master plan, but a remarkable beauty arises from the simple and authentic structures. The only sounds are the wings of birds, descendants of those to whom Francis once preached.

I walked down a sylvan path and came upon an outdoor chapel. Standing before the plain stone altar, all my questions faded away. A peace, perhaps a residue from Francis's time, came over me. I picked up a small stone near the altar. In the healing stillness I allowed myself to hear the simple song of the fisherman.

I put the stone in my pocket. It was time to go home.

14

I was unprepared for the personal attacks that began soon after we returned from Assisi.

For a year we always had several extra people in our lives because of our Romanian activities. We were all pleased when this period of intense activity ended. There were some delightful people who have become a permanent part of our extended family. Those of us who shared common concerns found ways to work together and to give support to one another. But there were others who were fighting battles that began long before they came. Much time was wasted with a number of volunteers. Some were unwilling to focus primarily on the needs of the children. Others were people who were prone to contention, afraid of sick children, preoccupied with special interest agendas, or not really committed to home care for children with AIDS. Many were disappointed we would not send them to Romania. In some, disappointment flowered into hatred and desires for revenge.

It is not surprising that many people would

have difficulty working with me. By nature I am gruff and getting more so as the years go by. This could be disconcerting if people came expecting someone who had an interest in the complex personal problems they often brought with them. I was obsessed with concerns about the children in my family and in Romania. Although I did not want to admit it, this was an unparalleled time of stress and confusion for me. There was no guarantee that the program in Romania was going to hold together. My grief for Tina was great. I have no doubt at all that these factors complicated my relations with everyone. It was easier for me to understand when I was the focus of someone's rancor. But often the enmity was directed toward Julie or Marti and, at least once, toward the children.

A woman came who wanted to go to Romania as preparation for a career with dying children. She had worked in institutions but never in a home setting. We were later told she was irritated by our grief for Tina. "They should forget Tina and get on with it." "It" seemed to be a numbers game. There are professionals who know how to do a few things for many children. We are lay people who are good only at doing many things for a few children. Our hope is that what we do can encourage other ordinary people to do the same thing.

After a few weeks with us, this woman accused the children in our family of robbing her of her self-esteem because they did not give her the "love" she received from children in hospitals. We were told she made a hysterical threat that she would stop us from having any more children in our family "if it was the last thing I do." And she tried.

After working with us for a few months, another young woman wrote articles for college papers acclaiming her positive experience with us. She maintained frequent friendly contacts. The following year a pregnant woman with AIDS asked Julie to adopt her child. When the mother was in the labor room, our former friend appeared and regaled her with stories of how horribly the children in our family were treated. She had decided she wanted to adopt the child herself and had papers with her that she wanted signed. Even after the baby was born and the mother reaffirmed her desire for Julie to adopt him, the frustrated young woman called the mother in her hospital room to say she would regret letting Julie adopt the child. It was painful for the mother, who was sick with AIDS and fear. She simply wanted to feel good about her decision. The delightful baby, Andrew, did come into our family and his birth mother became a good friend. But there had been a lot of unnecessary pain, which needed healing. What was happening? I saw a mother with AIDS who had secured a home for her child. And a woman who had just lost a child to AIDS willing to become a mother to another child no matter what the future would hold. They should have been allowed to feel good about what they did.

There were those who never understood the price birth mothers and adoptive mothers of the children pay. I was stunned to hear a man interrupt a mother's happy recitations of the exploits of a child with "But she is going to die. They all are going to die." He was saying "Don't get so emotionally involved." But that is the whole basis of what we were doing. A child has a right to own someone and have that person securely bound with love. When we would not cooperate in an ongoing relation with this man, he felt we had robbed him of his glory. He called up with a list of complaints and told Marti he did not want to be interrupted with references to dying children. He went on to take what revenge he could, attempting to find and expose any flaws in our life and presenting us as exploiting children and religion for personal gain.

People can become vicious when their personal programs are frustrated. It began to seem as if we were surrounded by individuals who were deceiving themselves and us about their motives and who had a passion for revenge when they were not praised and prized. We were warned that plans were being laid to take away our home by lawsuits, collect evidence that we were unfit parents, destroy our reputation by adverse publicity. "I have never talked to anyone so full of hate," one journalist told us after he had been contacted. The desire was to see us suffer. We are all very adept at making hells for each other.

Another person, who had known one of us long ago, asked to help in the sale of our Christmas wreaths and trees. She was cold and often hostile for the few weeks she was with us. We made allowances as she had recently been through a divorce and the breakup of her family. However, we were all relieved when she left. We did not realize her activities were only beginning. "I hate those people and I am going to hire a lawyer and get their kids taken away from them," she told a friend she was attempting to estrange from us. She made spiteful contacts with people whom she believed would hurt us. A letter to county authorities was perceived as harassment and ignored. Its author complained to the state, and the county was ordered to conduct an investigation. It was an ordeal as disagreeable to the investigator as to us. The county reaffirmed its support and once again the matter was closed.

I was becoming very angry and poisoned by all of these things. Objectively, I knew everyone is probably hated by someone. From a spiritual perspective, it should have been a time to reexamine my own actions and to forgive what needed to be forgiven. But I was not operating on a dispassionate level, and I often forgot my spiritual agenda as I fanned the flames of indignation in my mind. A Zen roshi once impressed me with a distinction between "big-mind" and "little-mind." "Big-mind" meant seeing what was happening to us from the detached perspective of Buddha. It involved taking God's view of creation. "Little-mind" resulted from being blinded by the mud that came your way. That was me—little-minded and getting littler!

The destructiveness of my anger became apparent to me in a ludicrous controversy over a swimming pool. Sister Marti had worked hard to have most labor and some materials donated for a pool. Everyone connected with the project felt good about it. The design is four connected circles. The first circle is only eighteen inches deep. The other circles are three feet and five feet deep, and there is a small heated spa area. It has turned out to be ideal for the special needs of our family. The children feel safe and most have learned to swim. There are family play times that transcend troubles. The health of all the adults had been slowly slipping under the stress, and the pool had an immediate effect on both Marti's and Julie's well-being. Since I have never learned to swim, my involvement was somewhat less. However, the story was circulated that we had built an expensive lap pool for me. The contractor, who realized little profit on the project, was accused of having persuaded us to build the pool for his own gain. I felt myself exploding with resentment toward the person spreading the story and the pawns who were believing it and passing it on.

In a fortunate instant of perspective I saw what I was doing. "There are people who love you. Children who need you at home and in Romania. Do you really believe that it is more important to focus your energy on what people who are not in your life say about a swimming pool?" I remembered the advice of the Christian mystic Meister Eckhart: "Think of your troubles as if they were happening to someone one thousand miles away." Okay, what would I say to a man in Canada who had a wonderful family enjoying a wonderful pool but who chose to be obsessed with irrational criticism? It seemed pretty clear. I talked to Marti and Julie. We called up the contractor to tell him how much we appreciated his efforts. Then the whole family went to the pool. We enjoyed it. Someday I may even learn to do a lap.

15

I do not have a tranquil relationship with the official authorities in my church.

The Roman Catholic hierarchy is often described as an "old boys" network. That is nothing new. Cronyism has always been the rule, not the exception. It was certainly a characteristic of the church of my youth. What is different today is that too many of the old boys have been replaced by little boys. An embarrassing lack of basic maturity is most clearly seen in sexual matters.

There is a chronic adolescent attitude toward sexuality in many parts of the church. Some church leaders are obsessed with other people's genital activity. Too many clergy have misused their positions of trust to abuse children sexually. Too many bishops have failed to protect the children. The clergy seems to be about evenly divided between homosexual priests and heterosexual priests. Perhaps this has always been so. But celibacy has become optional for a growing number of those of both sexual orientations. Many, including myself, see nothing wrong with optional celibacy for the diocesan clergy. What is distressing is the charade and hypocrisy. Also, sexual partners are often exploited, used, and discarded in a wounded condition.

What equally distresses me is the passion, in some ordained leaders, for domination of the Catholic community and the ease with which good people are officially marginalized because they differ in gender, theological views, revealed sexual orientation, spirituality, or politics from the leadership core of the church.

So why must I come to terms with a church whose leadership distresses me? Because it is my church. I am a Catholic. Not a "former Catholic" or a "recovering Catholic," but a Catholic, and I need to have an authentic relationship with the Catholic community. At times it would be pleasant simply to drift away from the organized church. I did once before. But no pilgrimage can be totally private. Personally I must relate, in some healthy way, with others who are attempting to pass to the next generation the story that was passed to us. The Catholic tradition helped me explore meaning and the spiritual dimension in my life. I am bonded to that tradition by the efforts and examples of my parents and some gentle priests and nuns. The bond has been strained but has never been broken. It never will be. As I answer a call and a desire for a more contemplative life, that bond increases in importance to me.

Like so many others who love the church, I have found that maintaining a relationship with its official structure is not easy. Cardinal John Henry Newman, the nineteenth-century convert and scholar, once described the Roman Catholic Church as "a cruel church." And so it has seemed to me. My high school years were spent at a Catholic seminary. For me, the experience was not a good preparation for a wholesome life. It was one of those institutions where the clerics could tell at once if a boy was the "right kind" or not. I was not. A few years later I tried to cease thinking of myself as a Catholic.

At the university I studied law and became an attorney. My legal career evolved into a concern for social issues. During the tensions of the civil rights struggle, I began to appreciate again the need for a quiet center to my life and moved back down a path with stops at humanistic psychology and Eastern religions. Eventually the path turned homeward toward the simple good news of the gospel I knew as a young child. Marti and Julie had pilgrimages similar to mine. Our paths intersected and the Starcross Community came into being. Contemplative men and women of whatever belief had much to teach us. Gradually we became comfortable with our common Catholic heritage. The window to the world, which Pope John XXIII had opened, was closing. But we did not know that. A friendly local bishop graciously helped us step back into the church.

As a community, we have an interdependent relationship with the rest of the Catholic world. Starcross Community is not an officially acknowledged religious society because, even though we are celibate, we are open to both men and women. Starcross is defined under canon law as a pious union or "private association of the Christian faithful." We make the traditional monastic vows but these are considered private understandings with God, not involving the hierarchy. We had assumed that both we and the churchmen were comfortable with this autonomous relationship. But AIDS brought to the surface a growing antagonism among nearby Catholic fundamentalists.

The American church was slow to recognize the importance of the AIDS epidemic. Before the bishops' first national statement appeared, public health officials had formed a consensus concerning the urgency of prevention. Sexual abstinence outside of monogamous relationships was urged as the only safe approach. However, it was recognized that such advice would be largely ignored. The condom was recommended as giving significant protection against transmission of the HIV virus during sexual intercourse.

The Administrative Board of the United States Catholic Conference, a body of about fifty bishops, published *The Many Faces of AIDS: A Gospel Response* in November of 1987. It was a compassionate document bringing a sense of solidarity between the hierarchy and the often lonely Catholic AIDS workers across the country. While affirming traditional concerns over extramarital sex and drug use, the bishops recognized that the nation faced a public health problem of gigantic proportions. They turned their attention to AIDS prevention programs in which the condom was being recommended, not as birth control but as death control.

Because we live in a pluralistic society, we acknowledge that some will not agree with our understanding of human sexuality. We recognize that public educational programs addressed to a wide audience will reflect the fact that some people will not act as they can and should; that they will not refrain from the type of sexual or drug abuse behavior that can transmit AIDS. In such situations, educational efforts, if grounded in the broader moral vision outlined above, could include accurate information about prophylactic devices [condoms] or other practices proposed by some medical experts as potential means of preventing AIDS.

The bishops' message was: It is better to abstain, but if you do not it is better to live than to die. There was an immediate, and uncharacteristic, public renunciation from conservative bishops. Officials in Rome, who were developing a strategy against birth control in Africa, were unhappy with this approach. Another statement was issued two years later by the full conference of American bishops. This new one said, in effect, if you do not abstain it is better to die: "The use of prophylactics [condoms] to prevent the spread of HIV is technically unreliable. Moreover, advocating this approach means, in effect, promoting behavior that is morally unacceptable."

Many Catholics working in the AIDS epidemic realized that in 1989 the bishops were approving the death penalty as punishment for morally unacceptable behavior.

The assumption was that most Catholics would ignore the hierarchy concerning AIDS prevention as they had all these years on the issue of birth control. As one Catholic columnist wrote in the *New York Times*, "I'm far less concerned about my kids' lifestyle than I am about their lives." In 1992 a Gallup poll showed that 83 percent of American Catholics approved the use of condoms to decrease the spread of AIDS. The majority of Catholic educators have quietly and courageously continued to follow the 1987 guidelines. But the condom became a red flag for the right wing of the church.

While recognizing the moral arguments in the bishops' 1989 document, a number of public health officials were angered by the statement that condoms were "technically unreliable." No one disputed that there is a sig-

nificant failure rate with condoms, especially if
they are not properly used. But many considered it irresponsible to suggest that the in-
creased use of condoms would not reduce the
risk of HIV infection. The issue was scientific,
not theological. The same point had been
raised at the bishops' conference during the
discussions preceding the approval of the 1989
statement. Some bishops had questioned the
wisdom of including the statement about condoms being "technically unreliable." But this
was an argument against condom use advanced
by some leading Vatican officials and the American bishops sponsoring the 1989 statement de-
sired to demonstrate their complete loyalty to
the Vatican.

In our local county, the top public health
officials were Catholic. Like myself, they had
expressed concerns that were quoted in the
press. We had a new bishop and requested a
meeting with him. It was an affable exchange.
The bishop observed that we were addressing
different audiences. He and his brother bishops
were talking to those who were able to hear
the church's teaching, and public health doctors were concerned with those who did not.
I left feeling that unnecessary future conflict

had been avoided. Shortly after the meeting the Starcross Community was quietly removed from *The Official Catholic Directory*.

It is necessary to be listed in the directory to receive financial support from some institutional donors. Funding for Casa Speranţa was important to us. We were there with the full encouragement of the Archbishop of Bucharest and the Vatican-based Caritas Internationalis as well as Catholic emergency organizations in Austria, England, and Sweden. We did not become aware of our removal from the *Catholic Directory* for some time. When I discovered it by accident, I called the local diocesan office and asked what happened. An embarrassed monsignor said the bishop had ordered it "because of the condom flap." A few months later Julie took a young woman dying from AIDS to speak at the local Catholic high school and the "flap" became an ugly tale.

Adrianne was twenty-one when we first met her. She had been a real California girl: captain of the university cheerleading squad, horsewoman, into every sport from scuba diving to skiing. Adrianne was beautiful, smart, and popular. Her boundless energy turned to AIDS prevention once she had been diagnosed. Julie became an informal manager in helping her talk to students. The students listened to Adrianne as they would to no professional educator. She was one of them. Being Catholic, Adrianne had a special interest in Catholic students. She knew she was dying when she asked Julie to arrange a final talk at the Catholic high school. Attendance was voluntary. The whole class came. So did a sensitive local reporter. The class met in the school chapel. The next Sunday's paper featured a picture of a pale but pretty Adrianne sitting in front of a crucifix. There were some powerful quotes in the accompanying story.

One thing I want to do before I die is spread the word as much as I can that you guys are at risk. . . . I wish some of your parents could be here, too, because that's where the education begins. Your parents need to know they've got to let you experience life, but they need to tell you of its dangers and let you protect yourselves. Otherwise, some of you are going to die from this, too. . . . It's so important to protect yourselves, so important that you talk about sex with your partner. I strongly believe that if you're not

ready to talk about it, you're not ready to
do it.

"That's the message I've been giving them
too," Sister Lilian, the teacher, said afterward.
"This time I think they listened." So did some
fanatic people who considered themselves the
diocesan condom patrol.

As fate would have it, a shy young woman
from out-of-town made inquiries about Starcross at the local diocesan office about the same
time as Adrianne's appearance at the Catholic
high school. The inquirer was thinking of vol-
unteering to help us, and her parents wanted
to know if we were legitimate. She later told
Julie that an older man at the diocesan office
became "very, very angry." He told her he knew
a lot about Starcross and gave her "a long
speech" in which he said he had "seen one of
the sisters passing out condoms at a high
school," and that "no one here has seen them
going to church." At the end of the conver-
sation she quoted him as saying, "If you want
to lose your faith and fall away from the church,
Starcross is the group for you."

In 1986 a former local bishop had publicly
described the Starcross Community as "one of

the more evident operations of divine grace and divine providence." Five years later a spokesman for the same diocese was reported to see us as a place "to lose your faith and fall away from the church." All that had happened in between had been our response to the AIDS epidemic.

The local bishop who struck our community from the official registry soon moved on to lusher pastures, where he promptly suspended a popular priest-counselor for co-authoring a book on the spiritual counseling of lesbian and gay people. Starcross was quietly put back into the official directory after the bishop left the scene. As the story of what had happened became known, we received private messages of regret and strong support from other church leaders.

It was a year before a new bishop was appointed. People who knew him described him as "pastoral" and assured us he would promptly set things right. I wrote to the new man asking his assistance on some spiritual matters relating to my living a more contemplative life. After nine months the letter was still unanswered, we had been removed from the mailing list of the diocesan newspaper, and again we were taken out of *The Official Catholic Directory.*

The church is my spiritual home, and the attempt by several officials to exclude us from the Catholic community has produced a unique heartache for me.

"Remedies," advised Cardinal Newman, "spring up naturally in the [institutional] Church, as in nature, if we wait for them." I wait, as do so many others. But in the meantime I must not expect too much from the hierarchy in my quests for God and peace. Recently a woman made a profound announcement in an assembly of people frustrated by years of rebuff from church officials. "You do not need permission to do good," she said. She is right.

"Church" means to me not the organizational structure but the community of those who are attempting to live out the gospel. My primary faith community is Starcross, which is a tiny facet of the monastic tradition. Therefore, to a large extent "church" for me is the Catholic contemplative communities where brothers and sisters have always reached out to us warmly as fellow students in what St. Benedict called "a school for the Lord's service."

For centuries women and men have used solitude and prayer to make an end run around the more troublesome aspects of organized religion. Monasticism became, in some ways, the first denomination in Christianity. Monks, male and female, often provided alternatives to the increasingly secular structure of the official church. The same is true today. Bede Griffiths, an English Benedictine monk, went to India in 1955 and assisted in founding a Christian community following the customs of a Hindu ashram. After twenty-five years he wrote:

Thus the Sannyasi [monk] is called to go beyond all religion, beyond every human institution, beyond every scripture and creed, till he comes to that which every religion and scripture and ritual signifies but can never name. In every religion, whether Christian or Hindu or Buddhist or Muslim, it has been recognized that the ultimate Reality cannot be named and the Sannyasi is one called to go beyond all religion and seek that ultimate goal.

I have long felt called to be a monk seeking for that "ultimate Reality" that "cannot be named." And, for over two decades, I have found my link to the universal church in one corner of the monastic household.

The Cistercian abbey of New Clairvaux exists in the agricultural plains of northern California. The brothers are really farmers. They raise prunes and walnuts commercially. But these are farmers who pray and are nourished by a centuries-old commonsense approach to living out the monastic interpretation of the gospel message. The long and unique relationship between Starcross and the abbey began at a time when the monks' quiet world was shaken by the changes in society and the church. In the modern age, was there a place for their approach to the monastic life? We came on the scene seeking what they were questioning and our presence became for them an affirmation. They had much to teach us about the monastic life and guided us through the writings of contemplative mothers and fathers. Through the years the relationship between us has deepened. The monks at New Clairvaux look at what we are doing at Starcross from the perspective of centuries. This historical viewpoint has provided a unique support when we have faced the many sudden changes of recent years. In the spiritually troubling times that began for me before the death of Tina, the abbot and brothers gently reached out in solidarity.

The Cistercian community is designed to be *schola caritatis*, a school of charity. New Clairvaux is such a place. The monks have encircled our children with their arms as well as with their prayers. They have offered us encouragement and, at times, helped us to heal. When cautious churchmen turned from us, the brothers took it upon themselves to reassure us that we were a part of the Catholic community and the monastic tradition. Here, for me, is the needed and healthy connection to the people of God I call "church."

16

The last thing on my mind when I was with Tina or at Assisi was unfinished business with the church or people who did not like me. I had a sense of my spiritual path and I wanted to get on it. These baneful cares seemed to encumber me. I longed to be free of troubles. But, at least for me, spiritual growth has never occurred in a carefree environment.

"Care" has been in the English language a long time. The Old Saxon root of "care" is *kara,* which is the word for "lament." As early as A.D. 725 the word "care" was used in *Beowulf.* But "carefree" did not appear until about 1800. Attempting to live without care is a decidedly modern folly.

Every person experiences severe troubles— things she or he would have done anything to avoid. When I have at last a vision of what my life could be like, I do not want to lose it. Just before Tina's last Christmas, she became seriously ill again. When Julie came to tell me of Tina's condition I remember saying the oddest thing: "This is the end of our family." Then I burst into uncontrolled sobs. Julie comforted me. It should have been the other way around. Seeking protection from the reality of Tina's illness, I had taken unusual comfort in the coming of Christmas. The family was joyful. Troubles were banished. Then, in a crashing instant, I knew that Tina would die and that the wonderful family surrounding her would be no more. There would be another family. Perhaps it too would be wonderful. But I just wanted everything to stay the same. When it comes to good things, I have grown weary of change and disappointment.

To be human is to journey from life to death and back. That journey must traverse some rough terrain. I cannot avoid the troubles. Yet I can choose how I respond to them. I am the only one who can destroy my life with fears and poisonous anger. I now realize that I need help at such times and that the help is always there if I turn from my preoccupations and compulsions long enough to be mindful of the solace offered.

When the worst is upon me, I often have been startled to find something of great value. Josh was our first child to die from AIDS. When he entered a final coma my heart broke. At the same time I knew I was not alone. Peace and sorrow coexisted for a brief time. Events of that sort are common to all people. The experience is so profound that afterward I question if it happened. Often I forget the whole episode. Yet it remains permanently in my spiritual makeup, depositing some wisdom to be called upon in the future. If I can find that grace in something as devastating as the death of a child, surely I can find my way through lesser tempests.

When I was a child, before people walked on the moon, the cosmos was a simple three-layered affair. Heaven was above. Hell was below. At times fiery lava broke through and flowed onto the earth's surface—providing proof of what is under the thin crust on which the living dwell. I am still among those who have wondered if our home is nothing more than the dome of Hades. There is no rational solution to many of our afflictions. But a simple response is found in a proverb from Issa's writings:

> In our pilgrimage across the roof of hell—
> let us search for flowers.

In that search I have found some precious flowers. There are Dana Rica and her mother Susan. There are the gentle and supportive monks from a Cistercian abbey. There are the people closest to me. There are people I have never met. There is the mystery I label "God." It is a breathtaking bouquet I am collecting. Sometimes I am able to step back from my own concerns long enough to realize that every careworn creature with whom I share this moment in history is also searching for flowers. That is our bond.

17

Susan Walsh Belfiore is an ordinary woman doing some extraordinary things. When she came to Starcross, in the fall of 1990, Tina's serious illness had begun. It was an intense time that brought out the best in everyone around Tina. Both Julie and Susan talk of Tina as Susan's teacher. Susan had never raised children. The plan was for her to go to Romania to prepare for foster mothers who were to follow. But our plans accelerated and Susan became the first mother. She was soon the spiritual core of our Casa Speranţă families and "Mama" to four special children, including Dana Rica.

After Susan's original time commitment she returned to her home and husband, Bill, in New Jersey. But she was soon back in Romania determined to adopt the four children and bring them to the United States. The natural parents of the children, the president of the local court, the American embassy, and even Bill's insurance company were all sympathetic and supportive. A waiver from United States immigration restrictions was obtained without difficulty.

Unfortunately, however, in Romania Susan became the target for a petty bureaucrat's frustrations and the quest turned into a nightmare. The official had little interest in the well-being of the children and absolute power to issue a needed document for the proceedings. For nine months Susan was the victim in a sadistic game that drained her mental and physical health. Contempt for children with AIDS was not hidden. At one point a colleague of the abusive official told Susan bluntly that treating children with AIDS was "a waste of medicine" because they "will all die like apples dropping from a tree."

I believe the rough treatment Susan received was partly based on jealousy and guilt. Officials were embarrassed to see a foreigner acting as if Romanian children with AIDS were worthy of love. They also envied the material advantages of middle-class Americans. Whatever the motivations, the official controlling Susan's case was determined to break her will. Susan was sworn at, humiliated, lied to, laughed at, ignored, and told there was something psychologically wrong with her. Time after time she made the arduous trip to Bucharest with hope and returned in tears.

Easter 1992 was approaching. In 1991 the Orthodox Easter had been April 7. Tina was still alive. Susan had gone to the Orthodox cathedral for the Easter service. When the flame of the risen Christ was passed around, she lit a candle for Tina. Carefully she protected the flame as she walked the long blocks back to Casa Speranţă. The candle burned until the day Tina died—April 9.

When April 9, 1992, came our thoughts were all on Tina. Susan was having an especially difficult day, depressed by the official disinterest of the government. Yet she took time to fax us a letter in which she wrote: "I have been thinking and *feeling* a lot of Tina today. I continue to be grateful for my time with her—she taught me hope." Just as Susan was writing these words, an official document was being signed in Bucharest. At long last she was granted approval to adopt the children and bring them home. There was no doubt in any of our minds that day that our little saint was involved in the process.

Months before, in an effort to keep Susan's spirits up, I had made a request. After Dana Rica arrived in the United States, would she bring her for a visit to Starcross? Susan had never answered. Things were too indefinite. A simple message was relayed to me as soon as she heard her ordeal was over: "Yes!"

Dana Rica was coming to Starcross! She was going to walk on the land Tina loved. A circle drawn in heaven was going to be completed here.

First, Dana Rica and the other three children had to come to the United States, get settled in their new home, get to know their father and grandparents, and establish a relationship with medical specialists. Then came other important steps: eating ice cream, riding horses, dance lessons, school, friends, parties—lots of parties. With each phone call, photograph, or video I more deeply grasped the miracle. Dana Rica was out of her hell. She was living and dancing and laughing. I would laugh and I would cry as I remembered our first encounters. The little dying girl I held was now dressed in a white dress and dancing around Susan and Bill's living room establishing her realm. Yes, like Tina, this child was a princess with very willing subjects. The doctors were more concerned about Dana Rica than the other children. Her cell counts were low and she had some troubling chronic ailments, including tuberculosis. But on the outside she was doing well. Two years before I was told Dana Rica would never walk or talk; now she was waltzing and singing. And, like the other children in her family, her smile was getting bigger and bigger.

At last the time was right and Susan made plans to bring Dana Rica to California. By good fortune Marolen could be with us at the same time. As I drove to the airport, I was doing all the normal things one does on such a trip. But inwardly I was exploding. Soon I would again be able to hold Dana Rica in my arms. It would not be in a stinking Romanian death ward with a breaking heart, but here at home with joy. Joy? Holding a child with a terminal illness? Yes, joy! For she was living and happy. She was able to be a human being, and that is a cause of joy.

It had been many months since she had seen me, and the flight had been a long one. I was prepared for a less-than-smooth encounter. I waited with the crowd at the end of the runway. Then I saw her. Susan had dressed her in a smart travel outfit that included a plaid jacket— one that had been Tina's. We were twenty feet away when our eyes met. Dana Rica threw open her arms and ran to me. I was ecstatic as I swept

111

her up and swung her around. She put both hands in my beard and sang "Twinkle, Twinkle, Little Star." Whatever troubles I had experienced in the past year were repaid at that instant.

When we got to the farm I carried her out of the car and onto our land. Our five children gathered around excitedly. Dana Rica examined them carefully as she had done when I took her from crib to crib in the ward. It was a deeply religious moment for me as I put her down and her feet touched the earth of our home. Here where Tina had lived and died, where I had agonized about the children in Romania, Dana Rica was laughing and walking off with her five new cousins. The circle was closed at last. It was such a special moment and yet so natural.

All the rest was celebration. Even when Susan held Dana Rica and cried in front of Tina's grave, there was a happiness in our hearts. Everything seemed to have a spiritual nuance, and so we gathered in the chapel for a prayer of thanksgiving. I stood at the altar where I had so often prayed for Dana Rica. Again she ran to me to be picked up. She was very still as I held her and recited once again the prayer said for each of our children when they came to us, the prayer I had used on the day I gave Dana Rica to Susan:

> *O gentle God,*
> *here is your child, and our daughter.*
> *Touch her with your spirit,*
> *put your star within her heart.*
> *Help her to walk with you*
> *all the days of her life.*

Those days were idyllic. David played his violin for Dana Rica and she danced. She also liked it when he tickled her and she tickled him. Holly was the same size as Dana Rica, and they were always together, exploring ant hills, swinging, doing things they knew they should not do but also sensing that no one was going to stop them. Michelle and Nicole enjoyed being older hosts for their special guest. There was nothing on the farm they did not show her. She met the cows and fed them. She played hide-and-seek among the Christmas trees. And she reveled in caring for one-year-old Andrew, giving him a bath and helping to feed him. To my delight, Dana Rica developed a passion for riding in front of me on our all-terrain vehicle as I gently drove around the fields. I would look down with pride at her holding onto the handlebars crying "Faster! Faster!" It was a father's pride. But I am not her father, even though Susan is always kind enough to refer to her as "our child." No, I gave her a father and mother. But I am a godfather, and I have pride in my goddaughter and all her brothers and sisters in New Jersey and Romania.

None of the adults had realized this gathering would be a celebration of what we had done together. Our focus had always been on solving problems when two of us met or talked. Dana Rica, with God's help, let us know that was not the purpose of this visit. This was a time to experience, as I had never before, the quiet joy of ordinary people who have tried as best they could to answer a call they believed had come from God. This was the first time I realized how incredibly restrained my emotions had been for several years. I had been afraid to give free rein to my fears, my angers, my despairs, and my happiness. In those consoling hours with Dana Rica, Susan, Marolen, Marti, Julie, and the children, my emotional barriers collapsed.

All things must end. Dana Rica was quieter

114

on the day she left. I was sitting in my chair where it seems I have held so many children in good times and bad times. Holly, Andrew, and Dana Rica were playing on the floor. At one point Dana Rica got up and came over to me. She stood leaning on my leg. Then she put her head down on my knee and watched the other children. I looked down at her beautiful hair. I saw the child with no hair I had first met. And I saw Dana Rica at six and sixteen and sixty. I rested my hand on her head and, for a long moment, I felt completely at home in the universe.

18

With Dana Rica's visit a spiritual circle was completed.

Native Americans have spoken of Great Circles and Sacred Hoops. The religious sense of the circle is an ancient tradition that has blossomed into many art forms. Complex spiritual paintings in Tibet are known as mandalas. In medieval cathedrals many images were gracefully organized into giant stained glass rose windows. I am beginning to understand that each of us must become mindful of the sacred circle within which we exist.

The circle of my spiritual life is becoming clearer to me. Out on the edges, where there are dragons in Tibetan paintings, are people I have disappointed or hurt. People seeking revenge. But there also are all the self-destructive tendencies of my own inner life. There are to be found the indifferent churchmen as well as all the bad spiritual choices I have made: pride over humility, security over openness, and hundreds of shallow diversions.

As I move from the turbulent outer limits

toward the center of my life, I encounter solid sanctuaries of peace; a portion of the church that nourishes, my family, memories, all surrounding an open space that is life and God. Each of these is dynamic and changing, and all require me to be alert and aware.

Prominent in the sacred circle within which I stand are the members of my spiritual family. I have shared such a long journey with Marti and Julie that the lines between our separate personalities have become supple and yielding. The strengths and gifts of each are shared and love often flows unimpeded by ego. Recently our community has been enriched by others. They call forth in me almost forgotten skills of helping another person grow spiritually. In the process I gain a renewed vitality of my own vocation.

The children are radiant jewels in the circle. David is bright and talented. He loves words and the violin, and is very good at both. Soon he will pass me by, but until then it is my joy to introduce him to life. Michelle was born addicted to drugs. She came to us when she was a baby of four months. A baby with AIDS. It was exciting to encourage her to give life another chance. Now she is a dancer. Our little ballerina has failing lungs and is only half the size of children her age. Every day she becomes more fascinated with existence and every day AIDS does its ruinous work. Nicole has come close to death several times as her body struggles with heart disease, epilepsy, brain shrinkage, diabetes. Yet she has learned to walk, talk, joke, get angry, go to school on a bus, make her First Communion with David and Michelle, and enjoy parties.

Holly and little Andrew tested positive for the HIV virus when they were born. This was because the antibodies from their mothers' blood were in their bodies. After months of emotional tension, the tests and objective signs indicate they are not infected with the virus. Now begin a whole series of other concerns. Will there be early cancer because of the powerful AIDS-related drugs the mothers were given during pregnancy? Already Holly has developed some precancerous markers. Has the HIV virus only gone into hiding, and will it reappear? But these concerns are for the future—and Holly and Andrew will have a future. They are both charmers. Holly is something beyond "hyperactive." Her beautiful voice can be heard through any known wall. Andrew is a big, delightful boy of Pacific Island descent who can demolish a room with incredible grace. Yet they both can sit a pony with remarkable poise. It is impossible to be surrounded with the sunshine of their lives without growing young.

Memories are sprinkled in all the in-between spaces of the circle: children and family who are dead but alive yet for me. My two grown children and the foster children and remembrances from each of their childhoods. Projects and accomplishments of which I am proud. Failures and hard times. Romania's children. Moments of peace at many places around the world.

At the center of the sacred circle of my life, of anyone's life, is life itself. I am comfortable using the word "God" for this realm into which I must now go.

The land was allowed to rest every seventh year in Old Testament times. There are still traditions of special years. Academics have sabbatical years. Artists and students occasionally take a *Wanderjahr*. Some years happen only once in a lifetime. Issa took to the road for a year after the death of his little daughter. I also had a special two years after Tina's death, but I did not understand until it all ended with Dana Rica's visit to Starcross. It was just like that Rilke poem:

> *And you suddenly know: It was here!*
> *You pull yourself together, and there*
> *stands an irrevocable year*
> *of anguish and vision and prayer.*

As far as I know, there is nothing before me but a very private life. I will devote the years ahead to my primary vocation—being a monk with a family.

I will live out the spiritual mystery of existence in my family. Some of the children will inherit the earth. Already the eternal vitality of

God is shining through them. They play music and dance dances I never learned. I know that something about the life we share together now will play a part in the future they face. That will satisfy me.

Others in my family will soon return to God. They have taught me much about the meaning of existence. Most of the issues I considered important in my sixty-three years have paled as I have learned to respond to the needs of a child on the threshold of death.

Everyone has to have a task. It is not enough, for me at least, to just be. Now what do I do? What divine instructions have been implanted in my spiritual genes? The tons of words I have read, heard, thought, and written can in the end be reduced to a few lines from the prophet Micah (6:8):

> *This is what Yahweh asks of you—only this:*
> *to act justly,*
> *to love tenderly,*
> *and to walk humbly with your God.*

Although frequently faltering, I have led a life in which I attempted to act justly. Loving tenderly is a pleasure I no longer allow to be sidetracked by cares and concerns. The guide-line I must learn to follow more carefully for the rest of my days on earth is "to walk humbly" with my God. Only in that way will I at last step through the broken window into a universe of stars.

The closing words of Issa's *Oraga Haru*,
written December 29, 1819

> *Trusting to Buddha*
> *Good and bad,*
> *I bid farewell*
> *To the departing year.*